VICKI HITZGES

STUCK ON ST**STOP**P

HOW TO **QUIT** PROCRASTINATING

simple truths®
Your Destination For Inspiration
an imprint of Sourcebooks, Inc.

Editing by: Alice Patenaude
Cover and internal design by: Lynn Harker

Photo Credits:
Cover: Mihai Maxim/Shutterstock; Sashkin/Shutterstock
Internals: page 1, Mihai Maxim/Shutterstock; pages 3, 4, 7, 11, 21, 29, 37, 45, 53, 61, 69, 77, 89, 99, 107, 111, Pocike/Shutterstock; page 6, Kumer Oksana/Shutterstock; page 9, Pavel Ignatov/Shutterstock; page 10, Pushkarevskyy/Shutterstock; page 13, Raywoo/Shutterstock; page 16–17, graphixmania/Shutterstock; page 18–19, Sergey Nivens/Shutterstock; page 20, Pixel Embargo/Shutterstock; page 24, Dylan Ellis/Getty Images; page 27, tukkata/Shutterstock; page 28, Nicholas 852/Shutterstock; pages 34–35, fluidworkshop/Shutterstock; page 36, Feng Yu/Shutterstock; page 39, Sashkin/Shutterstock; pages 42–43, Alexander Shalamov/Thinkstock; page 44, Omelchenko/Shutterstock; pages 46–47, Mila Supinskaya/Shutterstock; page 51, Mihai Maxim/Shutterstock; page 52, Rashevskyi Viacheslav/Shutterstock; page 56, Mike Watson Images/Thinkstock; page 59, TongRo Images/Thinkstock; page 60, Hluboki Dzianis/Shutterstock; page 62, Serhiy Kobyakov/Shutterstock; page 65, Elnur Amikishiyev/Thinkstock; Page 76, STILLFX/Thinkstock; page 67, Thomas Northcut/Thinkstock; page 68, gst/Shutterstock; pages 74–75, Pete Saloutos/Thinkstock; page 79, Warren Goldswain/Shutterstock; page 81, Picsfive/Shutterstock; pages 86–67, Ryan McVay/Thinkstock; page 88, DimkaSL/Shutterstock; page 91, Kzenon/Shutterstock; page 92, Catherine Yeulet/Thinkstock; page 97, Jupiterimages/Thinkstock; page 98, Natykach Nataliia/Shutterstock; page 100, Stokkete/Shutterstock; pages 104–105, fluidworkshop/Shutterstock; page 106, Peshkova/Shutterstock

Published by Simple Truths, an imprint of Sourcebooks, Inc.
P.O. Box 4410, Naperville, Illinois 60567-4410
(630) 961-3900
Fax: (630) 961-2168
www.sourcebooks.com

Printed and bound in United States of America.
WOZ 10 9 8 7 6 5 4 3 2 1

CONTENTS

DEDICATION

Not one to waste time, I've tried to imitate two men who can squeeze more out of a day than a circus can get clowns from a Volkswagen.

The first may make for an odd dedication, but I owe a debt to my ex-husband, Norm Hitzges. Norm broadcast the first major-market, morning-drive sports talk show in America. At the same time, he authored three bestselling books, traveled the nation announcing baseball on ESPN, and hosted TV programs for professional basketball, football, hockey, and soccer, as well as for horse racing, poker, boxing, and college football. He even broadcast the results of the International Grape Seed-Spitting competition. In addition, he was a professional speaker, made public appearances, and worked in the yard. I can still hear him cheerfully prod, "We've got five minutes. Let's get that ***done!***" I tackle more projects than I ever dreamed possible due to his influence.

My father, Dr. Haddon William Robinson, began preaching when he was a small boy. His congregation consisted of his cat, Topsy.

At age fourteen, he led twenty prisoners to Christ, and preaching became his magnificent obsession. His mind never stopped. Except at bedtime, I can never recall him idle. Even when he watched the news on TV, he'd lie on the floor and do sit-ups. No matter how late he returned from a trip, he would not go to bed until he had unpacked his suitcase. He studied, taught, wrote, hosted radio and television programs, preached, and led thriving organizations. Yet despite his many successes (as the president of two seminaries, the general director of the Christian Medical and Dental Society, the bestselling author of a shelf full of books and, most notably, as a fascinating, yet humble preacher), he always carved out time for our family. Always. Somehow, despite the constant demands for his attention, Dad made Mom, my brother, and me his top priority.

I'm also grateful for my mother, Bonnie Vick Robinson, and my grandparents, all of whom were diligent, joyful workers. They demonstrated (as I hope you do to those you love) that work brings satisfaction.

INTRODUCTION

The first time I remember putting off tasks was when I was a kid and we had to do book reports. The teacher would hold up a book and tell us we had six weeks to buy it, read it, and write a summary of it. Six weeks to a kid is like six dog years. It's eternity. It's so far away that the assignment might as well have been optional.

Except, of course, it wasn't. And those long, lazy six weeks somehow zoomed past and suddenly it was the night before the book report was due. And there I was, with an unread book and a paper due about it!

So, like many students, I read as much of the book as I had to in order to come up with a plausible paper *(not having any idea what the book was really about)*. The paper and I were miserable. Then, one day, a change hit me.

I was in the fifth grade, and for the first time in my life, I made a C. In fact, I may have made a couple Cs. I'd gone from vying for the spot as top student in Mrs. Clark's fourth-grade class to barely participating in the fifth grade. And the sight of those ugly Cs made me panic. I didn't want to be mediocre.

Neither do you. Procrastination, putting off tasks, makes a person ordinary *(at best)*. You can't do your finest work at the last minute. Creativity is a process. It takes time.

I learned how to stop procrastinating. When it comes to work assignments, I get them done. *Bam!* Right away. And you can, too.

What's more, you can learn to like it.

You really don't enjoy putting things off. It may feel good to snuggle in the bed on a cold morning instead of getting up to exercise, but it doesn't feel as good as hitting the gym and staying in shape. It may feel good to build an ice cream sundae and think "I'll start my diet tomorrow!" But nothing tastes as good as thin feels. And nothing beats the satisfaction of having the project complete, the assignment thought through, the task done.

So here are some strategies to get you going when you'd rather do anything else but work. *(One may be putting down this book and coming back to it when the job is complete!)*

The guidelines work only if you do. And the payoff is great.

KNOW WHEN TO

FOLD 'EM

> **"When you have a great and difficult task, something perhaps almost impossible, if you only work a little at a time, every day a little, suddenly the work will finish itself."**
>
> —ISAK DINESEN, AUTHOR, *OUT OF AFRICA*

Kenny Rogers had a hit song back in 1978 called "The Gambler." In it, he tells of a man who played cards. The gambler gave this advice, "You gotta know when to hold 'em, know when to fold 'em..." *(In the song, the gambler never said **when** those times were—just that you need to know.)*

I'm going to tell you when to fold 'em. When it comes to work, don't stop after you've completed a task. Surprise you? It's not what you think—there's more: ***Finish the task, then begin the next task before you stop.*** At least get the next task organized and ready to go. That's when to fold. When you're working, for example, finish one chapter (or one part of the research), then begin the next chapter (or the next part of the research) before you take a break. You don't have to swim all the way across to the other side of the new project, dive in.

This wise advice comes from, of all places, famed author Ernest Hemingway. The winner of the 1954 Nobel Prize in Literature used the trick to defeat writer's block. In *Ernest Hemingway on Writing*, Hemingway gave the tip to help other writers in his field. As he put it, *"Always stop when you are going good and when you know what will happen next. If you do that every day…you will never be stuck. Always stop while you are going good and don't think about it or worry about it until you start to write the next day.* That way your subconscious will work on it all the time. But if you think about it consciously, or worry about it, you will kill it, and your brain will be tired before you start."

So, for example, if you're writing a book, don't write until you're exhausted and your idea cupboard sits as barren as Mother Hubbard's. Stop while you've made progress, but still have the wind at your sails. My personal, additional advice is before you stop, scribble down a few notes about what you'd like to write when you come back. Then, when you sit down again, instead of staring at a blank screen or an empty page, you will have direction, will know where to begin, and can quickly pick up speed. Plus, you won't dread going back to work. Instead, you'll find you're eager to begin again because as soon as you sit down, you'll have both a place to start and a direction to head.

Keep Going!

This tip of going onto the next task after you quit the first task doesn't just work for wordsmiths. *It works for all kinds of people in all walks of life.* For example, my friends Allen Lindhuff and Ed Green work with computers. When they write code (a series of symbols, numbers, and letters), they finish one section of the code and then begin the next section before stopping for the day. Before they leave their computers, it's common for them to enter notes to themselves in plain English about where they're stopping and what to do when they get back. That way, they don't have to struggle to recall where they left off and it's easy for them to get back into the swing of things. They can immediately get back to work when they return the next day (or even on Monday after a weekend). Neither of them has to think, "Okay. Where was I?" As soon as they get back, they're ready (even eager) to work again.

Writers and people who do "mental" work obviously benefit from this tip. But Hemingway's advice works for those who do physical labor, too. Let's say, for example, you decide to paint a room. But, let's also imagine that you don't have time to stop right then to pick a color and start painting. If that's the case, don't just stop at the decision to paint. Do something! The first step is to choose a paint color. While you're eager to proceed, grab your smartphone and take photos of the room to capture the colors. Grab pillows off the sofa, swatches of leftover drapery fabrics, and a carpet sample and put those items in your car. That way you'll be ready to pick the paint color easily the next time you drive past the hardware store. While you're there, buy brushes, drop clothes, rollers, and painter's tape.

When you get home, start taping the windows. You'll be surprised at how much you can get done once you begin. When you come back to work on the project, the taping will have been started (or may be complete). Then start the next phase. And so on.

The point is, make it easy to return to your task without thinking, "What do I need to do?" because you've already begun. Since you've already started, all you'll have to do is pick up where you left off. *Momentum is a powerful force. Start!*

DON'T STOP
WHEN A PROJECT'S DONE.

STOP AFTER YOU BEGIN THE NEXT ONE.

*That's when
to fold 'em.
That's when
to walk away.*

SET A KILL

DATE

> ## 66One of these days is none of these days."

—OLD ENGLISH PROVERB

Motivational guru Zig Ziglar amused audiences who didn't think they could accomplish much in just one day by reminding them of how much work they usually got done the day before they went on vacation. Think about it. When you know you're going to leave for two weeks, you hustle. You get to the office early. Wrap up projects. Make calls. Dash off emails. Stay late and produce! Why? Because you want to finish assignments so you can relax while you're away. The days leading up to a vacation tend to ignite productivity.

The same is true of a deadline. Some people wait until the last minute, then stay up all night the evening before their project's due, trying to start and complete work they should've tackled days, weeks, even months earlier. Knowing that we face a deadline can spur us to action.

People go on crash diets and suddenly start exercising weeks before class reunions. Formerly obstinate spouses desperately agree to counseling when they realize their partner is considering divorce. Employees agree to take the training when they realize that if they don't learn the skill, they'll be replaced.

Deadlines get people moving.

I sat next to a university professor on an airplane awhile back. She had accomplished a great deal in her life. She told me she did it by creating *"kill" dates.*

I asked what she meant by that. She explained that her father had been a butcher. A kill date is the day that an animal is slaughtered. When you're in a meat market, you can look at the "kill date" printed on a package of meat to see how fresh it is.

"I decide when I'm going to 'kill' my projects," she explained. *"I force myself to hit deadlines.* Last week, for example, I told our dean, 'I'll have this project to you by Thursday afternoon at two.' By setting that boundary, I made myself accountable to finish the project by two on Thursday. The dean suddenly expected me to meet my arbitrary boundary. And because I knew that deadline was in effect, I lived up to it."

Note that the dean did not expect the work to be finished by any particular time until that professor set a specific moment in his mind. After she created the deadline, however, the Dean counted on her to get the work finished and turned in on time. And because she knew she had that deadline, she did.

Speakers who teach goal setting will tell you how important it is to put a time frame on goals. It's not enough to write, "I'm going to accomplish this specific action." It's also important to write, "I'm going to accomplish this specific action by this specific time."

Some of the most famous people of all time succeeded because they did whatever it took to hit their goals on time. *(And I do mean "whatever" it took!)*

For example, when the Greek orator Demosthenes composed his orations, he used to shave half his head in order

to look so ridiculous he wouldn't be tempted to leave his house to meet friends! Without television and radio to distract him and no one he wanted to see *(or have see him)*, he set himself free to work. And he did. He's still being quoted today. Demosthenes was the man who said, "To remind a man of the good turns you have done him is very much like a reproach." Sitting there isolated, writing with his half-shaved head, he wasn't distracted by the desire to socialize. And I'd wager he missed very few deadlines!

Neither, I bet, did Victor Hugo, the man who wrote the historical French novel, *Les Misérables.* Hugo did something even more startling to make sure he finished his writing projects on time: he ordered his valet to hide his clothes! He figured if he were naked, he'd have no choice but to work because he certainly couldn't leave home!

Obviously, these are extreme examples, but the people involved thought being half bald and totally naked would force them to produce—and it did! *(By the way, I'm not recommending that you try either of those methods, but if you do, let me know if it helps you hit your deadlines. If you get hauled off to the loony bin or spend time in a room with a cot and a metal toilet, remember when you get there, I did not advocate those tactics.)*

Professional writer Michael Geffner wholeheartedly agrees with the importance of setting and hitting "kill dates." As he advises aspiring writers in his blog, ***"Force yourself to work under deadline pressure. Deadlines are what separate the professional from the hobbyist.*** Pros can't wait for inspiration, or an act from God, to propel their creativity. They write because they have to, because someone on the other end is waiting for their work. They write whether rain, sleet, or snow, and all hours of the day and night. I've tortured myself to hit deadlines over the years, from five-minute ones to monthlies. That's the nature of the beast. It's where the tough get tougher. So, either get assigned to something with a due date or create an artificial one. If nothing else, it's good practice to see how well you function in such a situation. You may actually find that you're not cut out to write professionally, that in reality you're merely a dabbler. Not that there's anything wrong with that. It's just good to know where you stand."

*Work gets more urgent when others depend on you to finish. Get or set a deadline. Don't wait for inspiration to strike. **Set a kill date** and hit it. Half bald or naked. No matter what. **Finish on time. Every time.***

**Finish on time.
EVERY TIME.**

REMEMBER THE LAW OF

"GOOD ENOUGH"

> **"Better to do something imperfectly than to do nothing flawlessly."**
>
> —ROBERT H. SCHULLER

I have a friend who is slower than your child's piano recital. Slower than your *next door neighbor's* child's piano recital. Slower than a *stranger's* child's piano recital. **S-L-O-W.** He's bright. He's competent. *He can do good work. But he's slow.* He typically delays starting tasks, and once he finally digs into a project, he's definitely a three-legged horse in the derby. Slow.

One reason he's sluggish—and one reason you and I can feel lethargic—is that he strives to do things right. Or, to put it another way, he has a fear of doing things poorly. He has a fear of failure.

Psychologists tell us that methodical workers who delay starting projects and take their time finishing are rarely lazy: they're often scared. Perhaps you can identify.

Instead of working on the assignment on which you should be focused, you feel compelled to neatly organize all the papers on your desk. Then, you carefully print out labels for your file folders.

The truth is, ***some jobs don't need to be done well. Some jobs just need to get done!*** *(You don't need perfectly created file folder tabs.)*

Other jobs must be done exactly right. And woe to the man or woman who doesn't know the difference!

Don't be afraid to jump in and start a job. And start it again and again and again until you get it right. ***Don't let the fear of failure slow you down.***

If anything, *fear not moving fast enough!*

You don't have to take my wise counsel on that. Listen to the words of Jim Longuski, PhD, professor of aeronautics and astronautics engineering at Purdue University. Longuski wrote the intriguing book *The Seven Secrets of How to Think Like a Rocket Scientist.*

In the book, he says even spacecraft design students are afraid to fail *(which I'd think would be good news if you ever plan to go up in a rocket).* Longuski says he tells his students a story to help them get over their fears of not starting and making rookie mistakes. Here's what he says:

"There is a wonderful story in David Bayles and Ted Orland's *Art and Fear: Observations on the Perils (and Rewards) of Artmaking* about learning by doing. An art instructor tells his pottery class that the left side of the classroom will be graded on the total weight of the pots they create during the semester. At the end of the course, the teacher said he'd bring in his bathroom scales and weigh their pots: fifty pounds of pots would be an 'A,' forty pounds a 'B,' thirty pounds a 'C,' and so forth. The right-hand side of the class would be graded on the quality of only one pot. Their job was to make the best pot they could and turn it in for a judgment on quality alone.

"So at the end of the semester, guess what happened? The quantity students made the most pots *(of course)*. BUT—they also made the best pots. While the quality students sat around and theorized about the perfect pot, the quantity students were busy making lots of pots. The quantity students learned from their mistakes and didn't get hung up on perfection. Their quality steadily improved with the pots they made and they ended up surpassing the quality students."

Isn't that interesting?!

The students just slapping *out pot after pot after pot made not only more pots, but better pots* than the students who invested their entire semester trying to create one perfect pot each.

*Quit agonizing. Stop fretting. **Get after it!***

Go for it! Jump in there! If you're scared to try a new computer program, learn a new skill, or ask a girl out, *just **do** it!*

And, if it doesn't work out well, don't panic! Chalk it up to a learning experience knowing you'll improve next time. Then get back at it!

Try again. And again. **And again.**

Pretty soon, you'll excel at technology. You'll master the skill. Girls will flock around you like ducks on tossed bread.

One thing's for sure. As Zig Ziglar so aptly put it, "If you wait until all the lights are green before you leave home, you'll never get started on your trip to the top."

Everything doesn't have to be perfect. Get that pressure off you. You don't have to be great to get started. But you have to get started to be great!

"If you wait until all
the lights are green
before you leave home,
you'll never get started
on your trip to the top."

~ *Zig Ziglar*

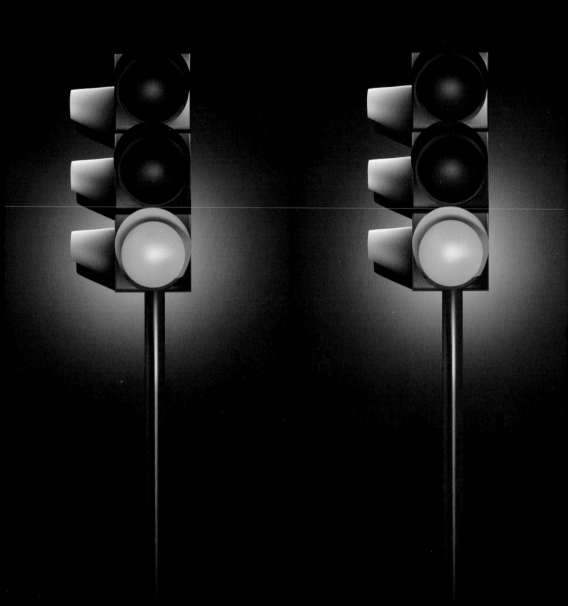

> ## 66 Nothing builds self-esteem and self-confidence like accomplishment. 99
>
> —THOMAS CARLYLE

In the opening scene of a thriller I once read, a small crowd waited to cross a noisy intersection. The sounds of motors honking, the occasional curse word from a driver, radio music, talking, and beckoning calls from hot dog vendors filled the air. The pedestrians waited impatiently, but then the light changed and they started across unaware that one of them—a man—had suddenly crumpled to the ground. Dead. One or two pedestrians who noticed the man drop stopped to help. The killer, a man with poison in a syringe, had quietly and quickly injected the man. No one noticed as he slipped away with the crowd.

When I think about that murderer, I'm reminded that there are silent assassins all around us. *Time killers.*

Like that murderer with the syringe, time killers look innocent enough. A harmless crossword puzzle in the newspaper. The inviting Sudoku game in the back of the magazine. An informative news feed on the Internet. Phone calls. Emails. Tweets. Facebook messages from friends and clients. Suddenly, your morning's gone. Unnoticed, innocent-looking distractions killed your valuable time.

We are often guilty of doing activities we like to do rather than activities we ought to do. We might actually work but still not accomplish what we need to get done. For example, scholars like to study; they don't like to write the paper. A homemaker may grocery shop but spend so much time reading labels that the house stays cluttered. Athletes like to run the winning play but may not want to meet curfew or do two-a-days. But to get ahead, we can't just do the jobs we like to do; we also have to do the jobs we need to do to succeed.

There's a way to do both. And a wealthy industrialist paid a lot of money to find out the secret I'm about to share with you.

About one hundred years ago, a man named Ivy Lee went to the president of Bethlehem Steel, Charles Schwab, and made a deal with him. Lee told Schwab he could increase Schwab's productivity as well as the workload of all his managers. What's more, Lee told Schwab he could help Schwab's executives produce a significant amount more if he could just spend fifteen minutes with each of them. To make the offer especially enticing, Lee told Schwab he wouldn't charge anything at all unless his advice worked. "Then, after three months," Lee told Schwab, "if my advice proves profitable, send me a check for whatever you think it's worth."

They struck a deal.

Here's how productive he was—Lee actually spent only ten minutes with each executive.
Here's what he told them:

"I want you to promise that for the next ninety days, before leaving your office at the end of each day, you'll make a list of the six most important things you have to do the next day and number them in their order of importance."

The executives were shocked that that was all they were asked to do.

"That's it," Lee said. "Scratch off each item after you finish it. Then go on to the next item on your list. If something doesn't get done, put it on the following day's list."

Each Bethlehem executive agreed to follow Lee's instructions. Three months later, Schwab studied the results. He was so pleased, he sent Lee a check for $35,000! *(That may or may not seem like a lot of money to you, but this was one hundred years ago. At the time, the average United States worker made $2.00 a day or $4,000 a year. Thirty-five thousand dollars was a LOT of money! Even today, imagine if you spent a few minutes with a group of executives and gave each one the same, simple tip and got $35,000 for it. You'd be thrilled!)*

Many people follow Lee's advice today. The founder of the $2.2 billion direct sales cosmetics company Mary Kay praised Lee's idea when she wrote the book *You Can Have It All: Lifetime Wisdom from America's Foremost Woman Entrepreneur.* Mary Kay Ash boasted that she herself followed Lee's advice. After all, she reasoned, Schwab was one of the smartest business professionals of his day. If he felt that bit of advice was worth paying $35,000, she ought to try it, too. So, each night she made a list of things to do the following day. But, she added a twist to it. She didn't just number the tasks in order of importance. She always put the hardest or most unappealing task at the top. "This way," she wrote, *"I tackle the most difficult item first, and once it's out of the way, I feel my day is off to a good start."*

Follow Lee's advice! Before you go to sleep tonight, figure out what you need to do tomorrow. *Write down the six most important things you need to accomplish.* Not only will you start tomorrow ready to go, but subconsciously, you'll also be working on those six projects while you sleep. Then, follow Mary Kay's advice and *knock out the hardest task as soon as you start working.*

Don't let your time get snuffed out by what appears to be an innocent killer! Stand guard. When you guard your time, you guard your life.

For *time* is
the stuff that
life is made of.

FIND NEW WALLS

> **❝I do much of my creative thinking while golfing. If people know you're working at home, they think nothing of walking in for a cup of coffee but wouldn't dream of interrupting on the golf course.❞**
>
> —HARPER LEE, AUTHOR OF *TO KILL A MOCKINGBIRD*

For many years, Microsoft's Bill Gates went into seclusion twice a year for weeklong *"Think Weeks."* Family, friends, and employees were banned from his retreat. A lot of Microsoft's innovations evolved from the "Think Weeks" Gates took every year. Facebook's Mark Zuckerberg and Apple's late cofounder Steve Jobs regularly planned similar retreats to recharge their thinking.

They headed out to fabulous, exotic locales to think and reinvigorate. While you probably don't have a company jet at your disposal, you can still change your environment. If you do, you'll be surprised at how much work you can knock out while you're away.

For example, many business travelers work on airplanes. They get seated and before the plane even takes off, they whip out their briefcases, grab a stack of magazine articles they've torn out to read while they travel, or switch on a computer and type. Other busy people go alone to Starbucks, the library, or a study carrel at a local college campus. They find a spot where no one knows them, settle in, turn off their phones, and work.

Megachurch pastor Bill Hybels goes to a restaurant and sits in the corner to work on his messages. He slips away where he won't get interrupted and can concentrate, study, and write.

It's very common for litigating attorneys to check into hotels a few days before a big trial and stay for the duration to concentrate on the case. They only make and take crucial phone calls. They don't read or send extraneous texts. Because they're away, they find they can focus completely on the trial until it's over *(and hopefully won)*.

When my friend Suzie Humphreys writes books, she often rents a small hotel room in Fort Davis, Texas. There's not a lot to do in this small town except write. So, when Suzie wants to zip through a project, she packs up and heads to the hotel and clacks away until she has a book.

You can head to a coffee shop, a park, a rarely used conference room—anywhere you can find where you can work comfortably without interruption.

You don't necessarily have to go far. When I switched from my desktop computer to my laptop, I started working in my bright downstairs kitchen. The sunlight streaming in the picture window makes me feel perky. I can turn off the phone if I choose, and just being in that sunny, expansive spot helps me get much more done than when I worked in my darker, less spacious office.

Sometimes it's good to leave your house and go to Starbucks or somewhere with some hustle and bustle. If you're home alone, turn on the radio. You'll find listening to something in the background will help you if you need to be creative. At least, that's the finding of a new study written up in the *Journal of Consumer Research*. Believe it or not, according to the study, if you're working on a project and need to do something innovative, noise will help your brain produce ideas.

Here's what I mean. Researchers from three North American universities asked students to complete a series of creativity tests while different levels of ambient noise, including voices, traffic, and other sounds, played in the background.

When the background noise was moderate *(about the level of a coffee shop)*, students scored thirty-five percent higher on the creativity tests than they did when the noise level was low. But, it only worked to a point. If the noise level got really loud, the creativity levels dropped and weren't as high as they were when the noise was moderate.

I don't know about you, but when I write, I like the room quiet. But perhaps I need to give moderate sound a try. According to the study, moderate noise disrupts your brain's ability to process information a little bit. *(Duh.)* But—that disruption causes your brain to work at a "higher, broader level," which, in turn, enhances "abstract cognition," or your ability to think creatively, according to study author Ravi Mehta, PhD, a marketing professor at the University of Illinois at Urbana-Champaign.

Don't get too carried away with this idea. It's great to do creative work in a bit of a din, but if you have to pay close attention to details *(like if you're suddenly called on to do heart surgery or when you're figuring your taxes)*, background noise might distract you. If, however, you have to figure out a great slogan, come up with a new logo, or write a speech, you might want to surround yourself with some scraping chairs and a few slurpers. Just be sure you're not sitting so close to people that you can follow their conversation. If all you hear is music, traffic, and murmurs, that's ideal. If you're getting the play-by-play of someone's steamy date from the night before and you need to work, according to Mehta's results *(and common sense)*, you're better off switching seats.

But **DO get away.** Find a new environment. A comfortable spot. Some sunshine, if you can. And a bit of ambient noise. The stimulation you'll feel will be your own.

Where is your thinking spot?

> ## "If you're the smartest one in the room, you're in the wrong room."
>
> —RICHARD TIRENDI

Choose your friends wisely. They'll make or break you. You'll pick up attitudes, skills, life views, and goals from the five people you surround yourself with most often.

Doubt that? Hang around a group of teenagers. No kidding. Volunteer to chaperone a two-week trip with a high school group and you'll come back saying things (*at least in your head*) that you've never said before, which means "you only live once." (*You might come back saying other, more eyebrow-raising four-letter words, too, but I'll be gone by then.*)

People as prominent as billionaire Warren Buffet, considered the second-wealthiest man alive, believes that his peers shaped him and that your peers will shape you as well. His advice? "Pick out associates whose behavior is better than yours and you'll drift in that direction."

Academy Award–winning actress Sandra Bullock agrees with Warren Buffett and me. *(I loved writing that sentence.)* When selecting coworkers and friends, Bullock says, "Always choose people [who] are better than you. Always choose people [who] challenge you and are smarter than you. Always be the student."

The English poet John Keats understood the benefit of a sharp companion. One evening, Keats sat in his study with his friend Leigh Hunt. Hunt read while Keats labored over a poem. At one point, Keats glanced up and asked, "Hunt, what do you think of this? 'A beautiful thing is an unending joy'?"

"Good," said Hunt, "but not quite perfect."

There was silence for a while, then Keats looked up again. "How about this? 'A thing of beauty is an unending joy.'"

"Better," Hunt replied, "but still not quite right."

Keats once more bent over his desk, his pen making quiet scratching noises on the paper. Finally he asked, "Now what do you think of this? 'A thing of beauty is a joy forever.'"

"That," said Hunt, "will live as long as the English language is spoken!"

Two things strike me. One, Keats had a bright friend who would thoughtfully listen to his every line. Hunt's wise counsel improved Keats' poetry and propelled him forward.

Here's the other thing: Keats get credit for writing the poem. But Hunt should share in the glory. He should at least get partial credit! Hunt sat with Keats until both men felt satisfied that the poetry was complete and finished eloquently.

Good friends contribute to our lives.

My roommate in college and I used to tell each other all the time, "I'm so thankful that you study!" If either of us had played loud music, constantly entertained friends in the room, kept the TV blaring, or tempted the other with fun outings, it would have made it much harder for the other one to plod through assignments. As it was, we both stayed home during the week and studied together. The best part? It was fun to study with a friend, and it felt rewarding to do well in class. Joanne Burger Cunningham—consider yourself officially thanked.

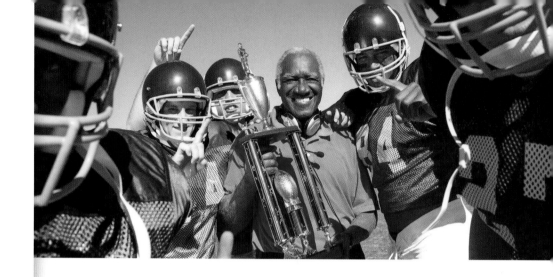

It's easy to go through life without seeking quality friends and colleagues. But your associates can make or break you. Because that's true, find people who will sharpen you, challenge you, make you better. Inept, uncaring people will pull you down.

Sports executives know that. My ex-husband is a sports talk show host and analyst. In his frequent conversations with general managers, coaches, and personnel directors, the names of difficult or negative players often come up. The world of sports is actually, from a total number of people involved standpoint, a very small world. Talk travels quickly and easily. Players move from team to team.

So do coaches, managers, and other executives. They carry with them information about players who are "bad actors." Those types suck the life out of a locker room. Their work level doesn't match that of their teammates. They're passengers, not drivers. Stories about them spread rapidly. There's a term for those players and their negative effect on a team in sports. They're said to be a "cancer." What an apt term! They're a disease. They suffer from chronic negativity and, when put into a team atmosphere, their cancer tends to spread to others around them.

Coaches understand the value of hardworking, upbeat, encouraging players. They realize that winning attitudes also spread throughout a locker room. Positive, hardworking players yield other positive, hard-working players. That's because we become like the people we surround ourselves with.

To apply this—think about the five people with whom you spend the most time. If they are not people with upright character, who push you and believe in you, I challenge you to find people who will build your life. If you can't find friends like that at your workplace, it might be worth switching jobs. *(Get a new job before you quit the one you have now!)* If you can't change jobs, join a professional association. Attend a church or synagogue and get involved. Invite people you read and hear about, who impress you, to meet for a meal or coffee. You treat the first time, ask questions, and collect some interesting new friends.

Want to win in the game of life? ***Surround yourself with people with integrity, faith, goals, humor, and a strong work ethic.*** *Like snuggling with a cologne-wearer, other people's qualities will rub off on you.*

YOU **WILL** PICK UP OTHERS' QUALITIES. CHOOSE YOUR ASSOCIATES WISELY!

GIVE YOURSELF GOLD STARS

When my father labored to get his PhD in communications while I was in kindergarten, he accidentally took the three toughest classes he could take—all at the same time. He carried a heavy load. Dad not only got through those tough courses, but also obtained his doctorate, with honors, by using a simple technique that can help you get work done. The technique is simple. Effective. And you can use it right away. The technique? He rewarded himself "if."

He'd tell himself, "*If* I finish reading these twelve chapters, I'll watch the ball game." Or, "*If* I finish writing that paper, I'll buy myself a roast beef sandwich." Other times, when he'd have a goal, he'd reward himself with something as simple as a walk or a stretch break. *(The reward didn't necessarily have to be amazing—but it did have to be something appealing that he wouldn't let himself enjoy unless he finished the task at*

hand.) Whenever he had something difficult to accomplish, he'd bribe himself by saying, "You can have that or do that or enjoy that if you finish this." He found that if he just quit working to watch TV, he got nowhere. But if he watched TV after he reached his goal, he got quite a bit done. Plus, he felt good about watching sports on TV without the guilty burden of a task looming overhead.

That tip will work for you. **Set a goal. Think of a reward that you'll give yourself only if you finish the goal—and begin.**

I can testify that the goal/reward technique works because without knowing my father did the same thing, I used work and rewards myself as a kid. I'd tell myself, "You can eat ice cream if you finish your homework." Or, "If you hurry up and finish your chores, you can go play." Knowing I had something fun planned worked as an incentive to get me going. I did the work, looking forward to the payoff. And, the reward felt even better than just ice cream or playing with friends normally would have, because it truly was a reward. It wasn't an activity I took for granted—it was earned.

I still practice that technique today. Depending on the difficulty of the assignment, I reward myself with a respite from work with something as simple as checking email or as elaborate as shopping for a new outfit.

Jerry Seinfeld, the comedian, does something similar, but his reward is more subtle and comes in the form of a red **X**.

The way to become a better comic is to create better jokes, and the way to create better jokes is to write every day. It's demanding and difficult to constantly generate new material. But Seinfeld does it. What's more, you can adapt his reward technique and use it, too.

Seinfeld uses his calendar to force himself to write.

He buys those great, big wall calendars—the kind that has a whole year on one page—and hangs it on a prominent wall. Then he gets a big, red magic marker.

Every day after he completes a day of writing *(whatever the stipulations are to that)* he gets to put a big, red X over that day. He told "Achieve-It!" blogger Brad Isaacs, "After a few days, you'll have a chain. Just keep at it and the chain will grow longer every day. You'll like seeing that chain, especially when you get a few weeks under your belt. Your only job next is to not break the chain.

DON'T BREAK THE CHAIN!"

he said again for emphasis.

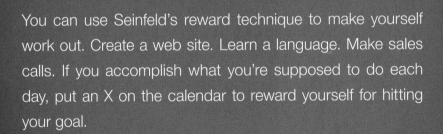

You can use Seinfeld's reward technique to make yourself work out. Create a web site. Learn a language. Make sales calls. If you accomplish what you're supposed to do each day, put an X on the calendar to reward yourself for hitting your goal.

Or, change it up. You can use rewards during the day to work toward an X at the end of the day. *(For example, you might think, "If I make twenty sales calls this morning, I get to go to my favorite restaurant for lunch. And in the afternoon, if I finish writing a blog post, I get to enjoy a glass of iced tea. If I make all twenty calls and finish all three blog posts today, I get an X on the calendar for the day.")*

You can use rewards to celebrate an entire week of Xs. When you have a successful week, reward yourself with a larger reward. *("If I get an X every day this week, I'll go see that new movie everyone's talking about. If I don't, no movie.")* Quite frankly, once you get hooked on Xs, you probably won't need the lure of a movie to make you want a fully crossed-out week.

Every day, think about what steps you need to accomplish to get an X at the end of the day. Feel free to reward yourself with small prizes as you tackle various steps throughout the day. In fact, go buy a calendar and start today to earn your first big, red X. Then keep up the momentum. Just remember—don't break the chain!

ALLOW YOURSELF A

SECOND CHANCE

"You may delay, but time will not."

—BENJAMIN FRANKLIN

Ever been on a diet and blown it so badly you thought, "Oh well, I might as well eat some of the cheesecake and restart my diet *tomorrow.*" If so, you might have a similar attitude when you look up and realize that it's one in the afternoon and you haven't gotten anything significant done all day. "Might as well go to a movie and start working hard in the morning." That's what my mentor, motivational speaker Zig Ziglar, called "Stinkin' Thinkin'." Instead, think, "It's 1:00 p.m. I still have four hours to really accomplish something today! If I use that time well, I'll get things done and feel great!" *Then, start!*

Not getting to assignments can mean not only a loss of productivity, but also can actually lead to heartbreak.

A speech professor once told me about a student he had with a great gift. When the man got up to speak, he was mesmerizing. He had natural talent. The other students in the class had far less of a gift. Because the man with natural ability knew he had so much talent, he didn't apply himself. He knew he was capable and didn't need to work as hard. Meanwhile, the other, less-gifted students listened, learned the theory, practiced, and completed all the assignments to the best of their ability. At the end of the semester, the students were called upon to speak again. Because they had applied themselves, the students with fewer gifts did surprisingly well. Then, the man with the natural talent spoke. By comparison, his speech was pitiable. The other students knew it. The professor knew it. Worst of all, he knew it. He realized he'd wasted the semester not working because he'd felt superior. He'd been lazy and arrogant.

After class, he visited the professor in his office and asked, "What can I do to make up for the work that I've missed?" The professor answered sincerely, "I don't know. I really don't think there's anything you can do."

The young man broke down and wept. He'd let his pride get in the way of his progress. At the end of the term, there was nothing he could do to make up for an entire semester's growth.

Don't waste your time. Don't let pride, laziness, fear, or anything else stop you from tackling what you need to do to succeed. Don't wait until it's too late—start now! No matter how much time has slipped past, begin!

START NOW!

Some of the highest achievers in the world enjoyed victory because of the effort they made at the end of the day. Here's an example: In the 1970s, Roger Staubach quarterbacked "America's team," the Dallas Cowboys. He earned the nickname "Captain Comeback" as he dazzled audiences by leading the Cowboys to improbable victories. He led the Cowboys to twenty-three game-winning drives. Fifteen of those twenty-three winning drives were comebacks in the fourth quarter, and seventeen of those victorious drives came in the final two minutes or in overtime. Staubach never gave up. Even when it looked like the game was lost, Staubach hung in there and, because of his effort, led the team to win after win after win.

Don't lose the fight! If you have a day that's slipped past you and looks like a loss, decide to come back! Make a winning effort now! NOW!

Before it's too late, stop dawdling, decide what to do, and START. You may have lost a morning. Even a morning and an early afternoon. Even most of the day. But start NOW. As Zig Ziglar put it, "Plan to work and work your plan." Start now.

If you know what to do, go do it! If you're not sure what to do next, after this paragraph, pick up a sheet of paper and write down what you want to accomplish. Then write down how you can accomplish it. If necessary, write down whose help you'll need. Set a deadline for each step of each task. Then begin. NOW. Don't wait until it's too late. Enjoy the satisfaction of getting things done! No defeat for you. Enjoy a comeback. End your day with victory!

NEVER
NEVER
NEVER
GIVE UP!

— *Winston Churchill*

"Plan to work and

work your plan."

—Zig Ziglar

THE BUDDY SYSTEM ISN'T ONLY FOR SWIMMERS

> **Friends in your life are like pillars on your porch. Sometimes they hold you up and sometimes they lean on you. Sometimes it's just enough to know they're standing by."**
>
> —ELIZABETH FOLEY

A few years ago, I took up speed walking. I walked with Bob, an ex-Marine, who had a sour attitude and a hearty constitution. No matter what, Bob showed up to exercise. He flew down the sidewalk! At one time, Bob held the record as the ninth fastest speed walker in the world. *He could move!*

I also walked with a friend named Ken Bradford. While Bob was serious and grumpy, Ken was funny and encouraging. Between the two of them, I started speed walking seven days a week. Notice that word *speed!*

We began walking in the fall. By that summer, Bob asked Ken and me to enroll in an upcoming race. It was scheduled on a Saturday morning. It was a fair distance away. And it cost a considerable amount to enter. *(Considerable especially because I didn't want to enter it.)*

But, just to make Bob happy, I agreed. Bob was a judge that day. I walked as fast and as hard as I could move. And guess what? I came in first for women in my age group! In fact, I came in first for women in ANY age group! *Me!*

Not only that, but I came in third in the race overall! Of all the walkers entered that day, only two men walked faster than I did!

Isn't that amazing?! I held *(and may hold)* the Texas Record for Fastest Woman in that competition!

I won a medal that hangs on a bright blue ribbon! *Me!*

Now, here's what you don't know: there were no other women in the race. And the reason I came in third is that there were only three people in the race. Ken. Some other guy. And me.

I lost.

But, I have never looked better from behind.

Every morning, Ken, Bob, and I would meet at the lake to chug around it. If it was raining or snowing or freezing outside, we'd meet at a mall and walk inside. We walked six miles every day at a clip.

Even on Sundays we'd meet. *(Not that I was happy about that.)* "Get up!" Ken would say when he called at 6:30 a.m.

"I have to go to church," I'd protest. I'd sound as regretful as I could, but truthfully, I was delighted to have a legitimate excuse not to go.

"Come on!" Ken would happily command. "You'll be done before the preacher shaves!" And, half an hour later, he'd pick me up with a laminated cup of lukewarm convenience store coffee, and we'd head out into the darkness.

The point is: I exercised. Every day. Every single day. I worked out because I had buddies who counted on me to show up. And I did.

At other times, I've worked out with Emmanuel *(an ex-con)*, with Brenda Bushell *(a TV producer and fabulous conversationalist who made walking and swimming fun)*, and with Anne Cameron *(a former Presbyterian preacher: Anne's liberal—I'm conservative. But we enjoy each other and like to work out. Or, more accurately, by 8:30 a.m., we're happy to have worked out.)* Currently, I work out with an ex-Georgia Tech football hero, Kenny Bounds.

If I didn't have a partner, I wouldn't show up as regularly. It's SO much easier to get out of a warm, snuggly bed on a cold morning if you've promised to meet someone. When temptation dogs you and a voice says, "Skip your work out," you might be willing to let yourself down, but you're not nearly as likely to let someone else down.

If you're tempted to put off a task, find someone who will hold you accountable. When my friend Ken Newberry started a strict diet, he told his friends in a serious conversation not to tempt him with sweets, meals, and drinks. We complied. And, knowing that we knew he was on a diet, he felt compelled to watch what he ate.

When I needed help with a video project, videographer Bert Newman worked with me, and in turn, I gave him leads to grow his production business. Working together, we talked about our projects, figured out ways to help each other, and got more done together than either of us would have alone.

Having someone who knows when you're supposed to show up, stick to a routine, or finish a task will get you moving and keep you on track.

Want to start a new business or overhaul your existing one? Find people with the skills you need and barter your talents for theirs. The secret lies in setting a schedule and sticking to it. *("How about if we meet on Saturday morning for a couple of hours? We can grab breakfast and I'll help you fine-tune your sales presentation. Then you can go over those marketing pointers you offered to give me. Deal?")*

If you get an accountability partner, you'll not only help make sure your work gets done; you'll also be amazed at the benefits you derive from having someone whose purpose is to help you stretch and grow. You'll produce more, learn more, and gain confidence. The more you do, the more you'll learn; the more you learn, the more confident you'll become. Knowledge leads to confidence. Here's an entertaining example:

In 2010, Cars.com ran a Super Bowl ad about a fictional wonder child named Timothy Richman. From his earliest years, Timothy displayed amazing confidence. His confidence came from knowledge. In the ad, we see flashbacks of his life.

As a toddler eating in his high chair, Timothy sees a pan of food catch fire. Somehow, he knows that baking soda puts out fires, so he calmly throws his rattle at the box of baking soda on the shelf above the flaming pan. The rattle knocks the baking soda box over, spilling soda onto the fire, extinguishing the flames.

When he learns to ride a bicycle, Timothy straddles his bike as his dad begins to put on training wheels. Timothy says, "Balance, momentum, and a low center of gravity," and with that knowledge fully absorbed, before the training wheels are even on, Timothy peddles his bike away and down the driveway.

In junior high, Timothy confidently walks up to a teenager on an Italian beach who's been stung by a jellyfish. Acting on his knowledge of first aid, he pours vinegar on the teen's inflamed skin. He explains in perfect Italian that vinegar neutralizes jellyfish stings.

As a high school student on safari in Africa, Tim uses his knowledge of veterinary obstetrics to deliver a baby Bengal tiger that was breeched.

As an adult, Timothy gets out of his car on a highway as a tornado approaches a bus full of cheerleaders. Using his knowledge of storm cells and tornadoes, he explains to the cheerleaders that they'll be safe if they exit the bus and lie in the low-lying depression beside the road. Just as the cheerleaders and Timothy jump safely into the ditch, the bus rises in the air and is carried away by the tornado.

But then, the ad's mood changes: We see Timothy's face with a terrified look. He's standing in a new car lot. The narrator explains, "When it came time to buy a new car, he was just as nervous as the rest of us."

Timothy sees a Cars.com sign and pulls out his cell phone. The narrator concludes, "So Timothy Richman got his knowledge at Cars.com, regained his confidence, and got the perfect car at the perfect price."

We're no different than Timothy Richman, fictional though he may be. If Timothy needed help to start a daunting task, so do we! We need other people.

Find someone who will be there for you.

Sharpen you. Teach you.

Build your confidence.

Get a buddy!

JOIN THE SOCK-FOLDING

OLYMPICS

A few years ago, while on a speaking trip to Wisconsin, I rode a shuttle from the airport to the hotel with a delightful, bubbly woman who trained people how to frost cakes. In fact, she was on her way to conduct a half-day seminar on how to ice cakes.

Because I love sweets and enjoyed her carbonated personality, I found myself wanting to know more about her work. If I weren't so addicted to sugar, I'd think it would be splendid to make money plopping and smearing frosting on cakes. Can't you just imagine the smell of chocolate buttercream icing just thinking about it?

"Tell me your best trick," I asked.

"Frosting cakes gets boring," she confided. "I teach people who work in grocery store bakeries how to make their work fun."

"It sounds creative to me," I said.

"Well, it's not," she countered. "If you work in a grocery store bakery, you can't be creative. You have to follow specific designs. And once you learn how to make rosettes and pipe, frosting cakes is like putting spackle around a tub."

"You've taken the glamour out of it," I admitted. "Why so dull?"

"Well, let's say a girl is celebrating her tenth birthday party and she wants ballerinas on her cake. Her mother will select the store's ballerina cake from a book of photographs. Then the icer has to frost the cake exactly like it appears in the picture. There are several designs—roses, leaves, the basket weave—but once you master the basics, you pretty much do the same old things over and over and over. You just follow the pictures. After a while, it's just work."

"You said you made it fun," I pointed out. "How?"

"Oh!" she said, her blue eyes brightening. "I **do** make it fun! I host cake-decorating Olympics!"

"Olympics?" I asked, trying to envision cake decorators racing,

each trying to outrun the other but losing traction and slipping on slick, brightly colored, frosting-covered floors.

"The Olympics are in my head," she said. "See, it usually takes a professional seven to nine minutes to frost a cake. So once they master a particular design, I time them. Then, on the next cake, I get them to outpace themselves. So if it usually takes nine minutes to finish a cake, the next time they might finish in eight minutes and fifty seconds. On the third cake, eight minutes and fifty seconds is the new record to beat. They compete with themselves. It makes frosting cakes fun because it's challenging."

What a great principle!
Turn humdrum tasks into games!

When I got home, I started holding the Sock-Folding Olympics. I dump all the laundry on the bed. I estimate how long it will take to sort all the underwear and tie all the socks together. Then start!

Timing myself makes that routine chore fun. *(It isn't a carnival ride, but it beats just putting away laundry.)*

It works with other chores, too.

You can time yourself when you're cooking, jogging, packing lunches, grocery shopping...in fact, it works on almost any repetitive chore that you tend to want to avoid (cleaning, washing the car or the dog, yard work, etc.).

Or, change it up a bit. See if you can finish composing that letter before the phone rings or you get an email alert or a text message.

When I have to wait in a long line, I make even that chore more fun by playing the Alphabet Game. *(I try to spot items that start with A then B all the way to Z.)* That keeps my mind occupied and helps me to not get frustrated. *("Aisle, boy, coat, diamond, earring, flowers," etc.)* Again, it doesn't turn monotony into whiz-bang, but it sure beats feeling bored.

My friend Kathi Ryan keeps her sons from procrastinating by turning work into fun. She gives them each a sheet of paper with a list of chores she'd like them to do. As they finish each task, they get to cross it off the list. When all their chores are crossed off, she lets them take their list to the fireplace and light the list on fire.

"Boys are born pyromaniacs," she explains. "Light a fire, you can get your sons to do *anything*."

The principle works with children, and it works when you have serious work to do, are under pressure to produce, and want to make a high-pressure task fun.

Todd Mount worked for famed restaurateur and horseman Norman Brinker as the tennis pro at Willow Bend Polo and Hunt Club in Dallas. But, in the winter, he had to get a sales job *(or, as Todd calls it, "a real job")*. He got a job selling gifts and accessories to specialty stores.

Brinker gave Mount some advice that Mount took to heart. He told him, "At the end of every day, give yourself a 'plus' or a 'minus.' The goal is to have at least five 'plusses' at the end of each week."

Mount set a goal for getting six orders a day. He was serious about that goal. If he got less than six sales one day, it meant that the next day, he had to make up for it. So, if he got four sales on Monday, he had to get eight sales on Tuesday.

Keeping that goal in mind pushed him. To his surprise, it actually made his job more enjoyable! He ended most weeks with at least thirty sales and at least five plusses. He also became an outstanding sales professional. Because of that self-imposed challenge, his determination, his sales, and his attitude skyrocketed. He'd made a tough job fun!

Think of ways you can turn humdrum tasks into games. You're more likely to do work sooner if you turn repetitive chores into tasks that feel challenging and fun.

EVEN AT THE STARTING LINE,

KEEP ENVISIONING THE FINISH LINE

A few years ago on TV, Staples, the office supply company, ran a series of ads that featured a bright red "easy" button. The idea was that you could hit a red button with white letters that said "Easy" or you could go to Staples and get your office problem handled quickly and efficiently. In fact, as you may recall, a company started manufacturing "easy" buttons. Unfortunately, all you could do with those buttons was punch them *(again and again and again)*. But they never did work. No amount of percussive insistence would deliver results.

Before you start a task that's going to take a lot of work, you probably feel a certain amount of dread. *(If you didn't, you wouldn't be reading this book!)* Few of us like to jump right into difficult projects.

When we begin tough-to-do tasks, we'd like an easy button. For example,

I just finished doing my income taxes. Believe me, I would have loved to have had a functioning easy button! But I didn't. I worked full-steam and then part-steam and then...took a break. It ended up taking me the better part of two weeks in February to do all the figuring required to get those taxes to my accountant. It was drudgery. And it wasn't fun.

Physical exercise is like that. I'm not a person who thinks, "Hurray! It's time to hit the gym!" I wake up, drink a protein shake, and make myself go work out. I try to make it more fun by working out with friends who make me laugh and push me, but delightful as they are, I'd much rather go to breakfast with them than to the gym.

Since we can't get easy buttons that work and since some tasks are just not fun, how can we make difficult tasks less arduous? Here's a good answer: to make a burdensome task lighter, don't focus on the task; focus on the result.

Let me give you an illustration. When you hit the gym, don't think, "Ugh. The treadmill. Those weights. That step routine I can't master!" Instead, think, "In an hour from now, I am going to feel great! And because I keep this up, I am going to get healthier and look terrific!"

Keep your eyes on the prize.

By the way, my dad called while I was doing taxes. Neither of us procrastinates. It was mid-February, and like me, he was preparing his taxes. He and my mother were going overseas, and he wanted to get his papers in order before they left.

He told me with a good-natured laugh, "I have papers all over! I thought to myself yesterday, 'Why did you start this!?' But yesterday, when I was in the middle of the muddle, I kept thinking how glad I'd be to get this done! In fact, today I called my CPA's office to ask when they closed and said, 'Don't leave! I'm going to finish this! I'll be there!' I knew once I had these taxes finished, I'd feel happy."

Whenever he'd get overwhelmed, he'd envision how grand he would feel to plop the papers and receipts on his CPA's desk with the task behind him, completed. And guess what? He finished! And just like he anticipated, he felt great!

And when I finished *(except for all the money I owed)*, I felt great, too!

When you have a chore ahead of you, don't focus on the work, the headaches, and the hassles involved. Instead, think how glad you'll feel when your house is painted, your desk cleaned out, your garage uncluttered, your checkbook balanced, your report complete. Then dig in…and begin. Whenever you feel tempted to get discouraged, think about the end result. The payoff. How great it feels to accomplish a dreaded chore. How satisfying it feels to get the task done. Then, do it!

By the way, I used several of these tips while writing this book. One of them was remembering how good it feels to finish a book! I also pictured going to the mailbox and discovering that the publisher sent a copy in the mail. I imagined thumbing through the pages and thought about to whom I'd give the first few copies. Thinking about finishing the book kept me from quitting. Instead of stopping, I clacked away on the keyboard until it was done.

The other end result I kept in mind was YOU. I knew that you could profit from reading this book. I hope you did. It was fun to imagine you picking up a tip or two and then getting started.

Here's to your great success!

I'll be eager to hear about all you accomplish!

Now get
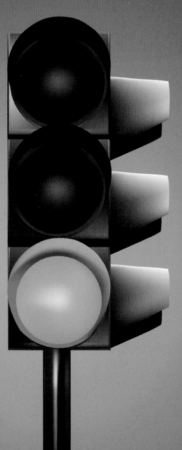

GOING!

No procrastinating.
You're no longer stuck.
Or stopped.

Go! Go! GO!

Photo credit: Danielle Johnston

"VICKI HITZGES"

—FUNKY NAME. GREAT SPEAKER!

Ever sat in a conference and nodded off? Your chin sank down, your eyes closed, and then your head jerked suddenly as if to say, "Hey! This is a meeting! Your dignity's at stake here!"

Next time, make sure your meeting planner hires a fireball like Vicki Hitzges.

Vicki delivers high-voltage, fun presentations with the stimulation of espresso. She never relies on PowerPoint to remember her talks or fill-in-the-blank handouts to keep her audience paying attention. She weaves presentations together with humor, stories, and activities that keep the audience engaged, laughing, and involved.

That's why her client list ranges from Microsoft to New York Life to Nokia Siemens to Chase Bank to the CIA. *(Southwest Airlines employees got so charged up, they carried her around the room on their shoulders!* **Literally!***)*

Vicki helps companies create cultures of encouragement. To do that, she teaches people to build relationships, think creatively, zap stress, and conquer change. She speaks from experience. She learned how to connect quickly as a Dallas TV reporter and talk show host. She can talk comfortably with everyone from plumbers to U.S. presidents. She can entertain a crowd of ten or ten thousand, and she's conquered a lot of changes along the way.

After being the first woman and the youngest person ever named Dallas Bureau Chief at KTVT-TV, Vicki became a publicist for several high-profile clients. One of those clients included legendary motivator Zig Ziglar, who quickly selected Vicki as one of a handful of speakers he would personally mentor. Within three months, she'd spoken from New England to New Zealand.

Whether talking about a moment that's heartwarming *(like what the elementary school teacher told her father that changed his life forever)* or practical *(like how the webbing between your thumb and pointer finger can affect your career)*, Vicki captivates audiences.

From now on, no more snooze-fests! Make sure your conference starts or ends with a bang! Book Vicki Hitzges.

www.acultureofencouragement.com
Email: Vicki@VickiHitzges.com
Twitter: @VickiHitzges

What OTHERS are saying...

"We purchased a Simple Truths gift book for our conference in Lisbon, Spain. We also personalized it with a note on the first page about valuing innovation. I've never had such positive feedback on any gift we've given. People just keep talking about how much they valued the book and how perfectly it tied back to our conference message."

—*Michael R. Marcey, Efficient Capital Management, LLC*

"The small inspirational books by Simple Truths are amazing magic! They spark my spirit and energize my soul."

—*Jeff Hughes, United Airlines*

"Mr. Anderson, ever since a friend of mine sent me the 212° movie online, I have become a raving fan of Simple Truths. I love and appreciate the positive messages your products convey and I have found many ways to use them. Thank you for your vision."

—*Patrick Shaughnessy, AVI Communications, Inc.*

If you have enjoyed this book, we invite you to check out our entire collection of gift books and inspirational movies at **www.simpletruths.com.** You'll discover it's a great way to inspire *friends* and *family*, or to thank your best *customers* and *employees.*

START
TODAY